Ducklings

Julie Murray

Abdo
BABY ANIMALS
Kids

abdopublishing.com

Published by Abdo Kids, a division of ABDO, PO Box 398166, Minneapolis, Minnesota 55439.

Printed in the United States of America, North Mankato, Minnesota.

052017

092017

THIS BOOK CONTAINS RECYCLED MATERIALS

Photo Credits: iStock, Shutterstock

Production Contributors: Teddy Borth, Jennie Forsberg, Grace Hansen

Design Contributors: Christina Doffing, Candice Keimig, Dorothy Toth

Publisher's Cataloging in Publication Data

Names: Murray, Julie, 1969-, author.

Title: Ducklings / by Julie Murray.

Description: Minneapolis, Minnesota : Abdo Kids, 2018 | Series: Baby animals | Includes bibliographical references and index.

Identifiers: LCCN 2016962291 | ISBN 9781532100017 (lib. bdg.) | ISBN 9781532100703 (ebook) | ISBN 9781532101250 (Read-to-me ebook)

Subjects: LCSH: Ducklings--Juvenile literature. | Ducklings--Infancy--Juvenile literature.

Classification: DDC 598.4--dc23

LC record available at http://lccn.loc.gov/2016962291

Table of Contents

Ducklings 4

Watch a Mallard Duck Grow! 22

Glossary 23

Index 24

Abdo Kids Code 24

Ducklings

A baby duck is a duckling.

Ducklings **hatch** from eggs.

They are small.

They have **beaks**.

They have fluffy feathers.

These keep them warm.

They also keep them dry.

They have **webbed** feet.

These help them swim.

They make a “cheep” sound.

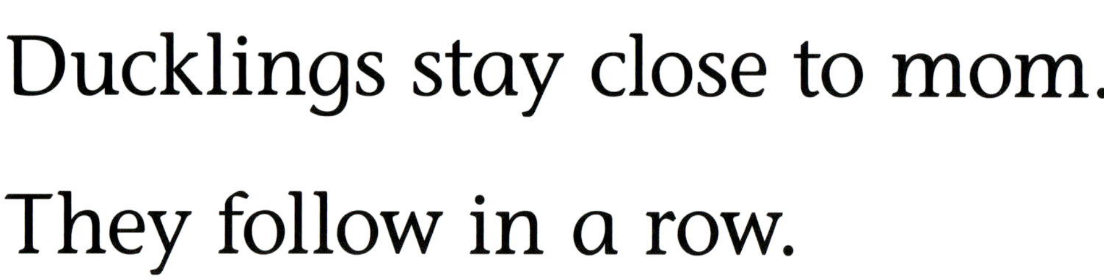
Ducklings stay close to mom.

They follow in a row.

They eat insects.

They also eat plants.

Soon they will be able to fly!

Watch a Mallard Duck Grow!

newborn

1 month

4 months

1 year

Glossary

beak
the strong, hard bill of a bird.

hatch
to be born from an egg.

webbed
having fingers or toes connected by skin.

Index

baby 4

beak 8

duck 4

egg 6

feathers 10

feet 12

fly 20

food 18

mom 16

sound 14

abdokids.com

Use this code to log on to abdokids.com and access crafts, games, videos, and more!

Abdo Kids Code:
BDK0017